A Few of My Favorites

Layered Bean Stew
Stewed Beef
Curry Goat
Seared Oven Roasted Beef
Poached Salmon & Eggs
Mediterranean Chicken
Garlic Butter Shrimp
Creamy Shrimp Bisque
Chicken Salad Wraps
Soup & Sandwich
Seafood & Pasta
Cayne's Avocado Bagel

Volume II features even more dishes from Cayne's Kitchen. The above list is just a few meals of what comes through my kitchen. I love seafood and Caribbean food and as such i mesh the two worlds together to create an amazing and delicious meal.

Cayne's Kitchen Volume II is a follow up edition. I had so much fun creating Volume I that I couldn't wait to start cooking and writing again for Volume II. Just as before, this volume will include traditional style dishes with West Indian culture infused with the Southern influence that have become my family.

I was blessed to be born on the Island of St. Croix USVI with family all across the West Indies. It is that Island culture that fuels my curiosity and creativity while in the kitchen, in fact the very one thing I do while cooking is listening to music. It is not uncommon to walk into my home and find me dashing around the kitchen and singing and dancing to my reggae or calypso music. I always tell my children when the cook is happy the food will always taste great.

To understand my cooking you must first understand my background. I am the youngest of 10 children however many of my siblings are much older than me so quite naturally I was able to witness different styles of cooking.

From a small boy I spent many a days watching my mother or father cook in the kitchen. Sometimes my mother would cook baked chicken with peas and rice and on the weekends my father would make salt-fish, a traditional Island meal. These are the origins of where the love for cooking started.

Poached Swai and Eggs

(Measurements are in 1 to 2 tsp and tbsp., and 1 cup. Season to your own taste using this guide)
Swai fish or other fish (Trout, Tilapia, etc.)
Salt & pepper
Garlic powder
Onion Powder
Seafood stock
Old bay
Fresh herbs – rosemary, thyme, dill weed
Onion
Peppers (green, red, or yellow)
Eggs

In a large pan fill with water and add:
All the above seasonings
Bring to seasoned water to a boil
Add fish to the water and submerge
Reduce heat to low to medium
Cook for about 15 to 20 minutes or until fish becomes flaky

In a separate pan cook eggs as desired (fried, scrambled, or poached)
Serve fish besides eggs

Pan Seared Trout w/Spinach

(Measurements are in 1 to 2 tsp and tbsp., and 1 cup.
Season to your own taste using this guide)
Trout fish or other fish (Swai, Tilapia, etc.)
Salt & pepper
Garlic powder
Onion Powder
Fresh herbs – rosemary, thyme, dill weed
Onion
Peppers (green, red, or yellow)

Pan searing fish is delicate
Season fish on both sides
add oil to non stick pan over medium heat
Sear fish on both sides for 5 minutes or until edges become crisp

Serve fish with sautéed spinach

Loaded Seafood Potato

(Measurements are in 1 to 2 tsp and tbsp., and 1 cup. Season to your own taste using this guide)
Shrimp
Small lobster tail
Crab-meat
Onion
Broccoli
Peppers
Sour cream
Salt & Pepper
Olive oil
Butter
Bake potato(s)

Wash and dry bake potato
Preheat oven to 350 degrees
Coat potato with olive oil and sprinkle with salt
Place in oven in middle rack and bake for about an hour or until done
Boil lobster tails for about 3-5 minutes, until shell turns red (depending on size – add more time)
Boil shrimp and remove shell
In a separate dish mix the sour cream, chopped lobster tail, shrimp, crab meat, and broccoli
Place iron skillet over medium heat; Add olive oil; Add in chopped onion and peppers
Add butter and sauté until translucent
Add onions and peppers to sour cream mix; Add in cheese and combine mixture
Remove potato(s) from oven and make a slit down the top middle
Allow to cool; Scoop potato out the middle
Scoop in the sour cream mixture to your bake potato
Place back in oven for 15 minutes

The "Bean King"

Ever since I could remember I've always had some sort of bean or pea in my diet. My mom used to make peas and rice with almost every meal, it's an Island thing I guess. So naturally once I met my wife's family and they were feeding me red beans and rice, I was already used to it. Over the years I've developed my own way and style of cooking beans, so much so my wife has crowned me the bean king in the house. It's now a joke in my home that whenever I am cooking beans no one can witness the herbs and spices I use to make them, my wife hates it but loves it when I'm done. Even my youngest son says my beans and rice are his favorite, I'm not sure if he's pulling my chain but it feels good hearing it anyway.

Two Layer Bean Casserole

(Measurements are in 1 to 2 tsp and tbsp., and 1 cup.
Season to your own taste using this guide)
Black bean, Kidney Bean
Salt & pepper
Garlic powder
Onion Powder
Vegetable stock
Onion
Peppers (green, red, or yellow)

In a large pan add olive oil over medium heat
sautee fresh garlic, onions, and peppers
Sautee until vegetables become translucent
Add in the beans and cook in for about 5 minutes covered
Combine stock and water and add to beans
Cover and allow to simmer
Smash a few beans against the potato thicken the sauce
Taste for additional seasoning needed
Add in tomatoes and broccoli
Cook until beans are tender

Pan Seared BBQ Chicken w/Caesar salad

(Measurements are in 1 to 2 tsp and tbsp., and 1 cup.
Season to your own taste using this guide)
Leg Quarters, split or whole
Salt & pepper
Garlic powder
Onion Powder
Fresh herbs – rosemary, thyme
Onion
Peppers (green, red, or yellow)

Clean chicken thoroughly in vinegar and water
Pat chicken dry
Add all seasoning to chicken and combine evenly
Add oil to the pan over medium heat
Place skin side down and allow to sear until skin gets browned
Flip and sear on other side
Add your favorite BBQ sauce to the chicken
Do not cover chicken

Serve next to Caesars salad

St. Lucia

Creamy Shrimp Bisque

(Measurements are in 1 to 2 tsp and tbsp., and 1 cup. Season to your own taste using this guide)

2-4 Potatoes
1 cup cubed butternut squash
1 large white onion
1 large red onion
2-4 clove garlic
2 table spoons all-purpose flower
½ cup milk or heavy cream
1 cup seafood broth
2 strips bacon
Salt & pepper
i cup salad shrimp
1/2 pound large shrimp
Cajun seasoning

In a medium to large pan cook ba
When bacon is fully cooked remove and set aside
Chop white onions and garlic
Place onion and garlic in bacon grease and cook down until onion is translucent
Pour in seafood broth and stir to mix thoroughly
In small pot add flower and pour in milk – mix until smooth
Pour flower mixture into pot with seafood broth
Add potatoes
Turn heat down to low and cover
Cook for about 20-30 minutes
Pour half of the soup into a food compressor and pulse until liquid is smooth
Add cooked salad shrimp to soup
In other pan, pan sear large shrimp in Cajun seasoning
Pour back into pot and stir with remaining soup
Add salt and pepper to taste
Garnish with your choice of cheese, red onion, and remaining bacon

Spicy Bourbon Swai & Shrimp Caesars Salad

(Measurements are in 1 to 2 tsp and tbsp., and 1 cup. Season to your own taste using this guide)
Swai fish or other fish (salmon, Tilapia, etc.)
Shrimp
Salt & pepper
Garlic powder
Onion Powder
Olive oil

Sauce:
½ cup brown sugar
3 tablespoons Worcestershire sauce
1 teaspoon cayenne pepper
Dash of salt & ground pepper
½ cup ketchup
1 teaspoon of mustard (dried mustard can be used also)
1/3 cup Bourbon Whiskey
2 tablespoons balsamic vinegar

Bourbon sauce:
In a bowl add brown sugar, ketchup, mustard, Worcestershire sauce, vinegar, cayenne pepper, salt, and bourbon
Mix well and set aside
Rinse fish and pat dry
Season both sides with salt, pepper, and garlic powder
Preheat oven to 350 degrees
Coat a thin layer of olive oil in a baking dish
Arrange fish in baking dish and bake uncovered for 15-20 minutes
After 15 minutes pour bourbon sauce over fish and place back in the oven until sauce begins to bubble
While fish is in the oven peel shrimp down to the tail
On the stove top set heat to medium
Add 3 tablespoons of butter
When butter has melted add the shrimp and toss
Pour bourbon mixture over the shrimp
Cover and simmer until shrimp are fully cooked
When both fish and shrimp are fully cooked serve over Caesars salad or fresh vegetables

My inspiration for cooking and creating these lovely meals comes with a partner. I dare not say it is second to anything because it really stands on its own. My other love, if you hadn't figured it out yet is photography. Infused all throughout this book are photos I've taken in my own city or when I travel and visit other cities. When traveling on business I always pack one of three cameras; like my American Express, I never leave home without at least one.

Cooking for many people is a hassle but for me it's my quiet time, my peaceful time. Like a mad man I have everything going off in my head like do I have all the seasonings I need, how long shall something bake or sear, reminding myself not to over salt the meat.

I say that jokingly because my wife is the "salt" police, she can taste salt in everything and will be the first person to let me know if my hand gets away with salt or any other seasoning. I say this lovingly, I know she is looking out for my health and in turn looks out for everyone who enjoys my meals.

Photography gives me the same freedom to create like cooking does. Each one of the images you see in this book was carefully shot by me and once I reviewed the image I already had in mind how I was going to process it. When I began thinking about Volume II I said to myself how can I join my two loves and have them work together. No sooner than I had the thought the idea of black & white images around robust colorful dishes became my working theme.

Pan Seared Mackerel over
sauteed onions & peppers

Avocado & Tomato Bruschetta

Boordy Winery Baltimore MD

Cheesy Crab Mac & Cheese

(Measurements are in 1 to 2 tsp and tbsp.,
and 1 cup. Season to your own taste using this guide)
Crab meat
Elbow macaroni
Butter
Sour cream
2 eggs
Whipping cream
Cajun seasoning
Cheeses: cheddar, pepper jack

Boil elbow macaroni per box instructions (5-7 minutes)
In a large bowl grate cheeses (3-4 cups)
In another bowl mix:
2 eggs
1 cup whipping cream
1/3 cup sour cream
Add Cajun seasoning
Mix is crab meat or (you can use a crab dip mixture pre-made)
Strain pasta and mix in well with crab meat and cheese mixture
Preheat oven to 350 degrees
Butter pan baking dish
Pour pasta mixture into baking dish
Sprinkle with remaining cheese
Bake for 45 minutes to 1 hour or until cheese has browned and bubbly

Marriott Phoenix Arizona

Phoenix Arizona is one of my favorite places to visit. There are so many cultural likes in and around the city it will satisfy any taste you might have. When I found myself in AZ for a week I experienced Tex-Mex, Asian, Hawaii, BBQ, All styles of delicious pizza, needless to say I was stuffed.

My travels took me all through Phoenix, Mesa, Scottsdale, Flagstaff, and Sedona. Each area has its own authentic cultural differences and style of food. From delectable steaks to spicy Mexican to seafood that will make your head spin.

If you're ever in this area I suggest spending some time in one of the areas most wonderful and soothing spas, I surely did!

Bourbon Chicken with Butternut Squash

(Measurements are in 1 to 2 tsp and tbsp., and 1 cup.
Season to your own taste using this guide)
Leg Quarters, split or whole
Salt & pepper
Garlic powder
Onion Powder
Fresh herbs – rosemary, thyme, ginger
Onion
Peppers (green, red, or yellow)
Bourbon
BBQ sauce

Clean chicken thoroughly in vinegar and water
Pat chicken dry
Add all seasoning to chicken and combine evenly
Add oil to the pan over medium heat
Place skin side down and allow to sear until skin gets browned
Flip and sear on other side
Add BBQ Bourbon sauce to the chicken
Flip and sear skin side down before removing from pan
Do not cover chicken

Serve next to Caesars salad

Elkridge Community Chicago ILL

Rosemary Oven Stuffer

Each year I travel on business to the lovely city of Chicago. This year while there I ate at a place where they served a tender fillet mignon with garlic and roasted nuts. I loved the idea so much that when I returned to my home town I crushed some garlic, added olive oil, and crushed some pecans in a food processor then poured the newly garlic pecan olive oil into a jar.

Ingredients:
My olive mix
8-10 lb roaster
Red onions
Red bell peppers
Potatoes
Rosemary
Salt & pepper
to taste

Wash and clean bird with cold water
Pat dry
Rub the olive oil mix all oven the bird, inside and out
Season bird with salt, pepper, and rosemary
Stuff bird with onions, peppers, and potatoes
Baked covered for 90 min, uncover last 30 min.

I'm an IT Professional by day and creative spirit by night. Over the past 20 or so years I have owned and operated a web design company, a computer repair shop, modeling and photography studio, and designed and distributed a small print magazine called NFLAVA. I have been blessed with many talents including the love for creating and plating a scrumptious meal. I am really big on presentation. I find most dishes are deemed tasty from just sight alone. Adversely, a messy plate or junkie unorganized restaurant will be seen as having not so good food.

The concept of this cook book came to me as an idea I had of combining the 2 loves I have in life, one being cooking of course, but the other being my photography. Throughout this book I've shared parts of my journey as a cook and as a photographer. Some of the shots seen are from various cities such as Chicago, Seattle, Virginia, Baltimore, Atlanta, Pittsburgh, and many many more. A few are select images taken while traveling across the West Indies.

I hope you can sit back and enjoy my journey through my travels, photography, and great foods.

Tender Roast Beef atop Fresh Kale & Creamy Garlic Mash Potatoes

(Measurements are in 1 to 2 tsp and tbsp., and 1 cup.
Season to your own taste using this guide)
Shoulder Roast
Salt & pepper
Garlic powder
Onion Powder
Cream cheese
Milk or Whipping cream
Butter
Potatoes
Fresh herbs – rosemary, thyme

Rinse shoulder roast thoroughly with water
Pat dry and combine seasonings
Rub dry seasoning all over roast
Cover and allow to sit refrigerated for at least an hour
Remove from refrigerator and let sit for 5-10 minutes
Preheat oven to 350 degrees
Place roast in a lightly oiled oven roaster; covered
Roast for 2 hours; check for tenderness
Continue to roast until desired tenderness is reached

In a pot of boiling water, skin on or skin off, add potatoes
Boil until tender and soft
Remove water
Add garlic, butter, and salt
Add 3 tablespoons of cream cheese
Add 1/3 cup of milk or whipping cream
Mix until desired smoothness is reached
Serve next to Caesars salad

Fort Washington MD

Curry Goat w/rice & beans

(Measurements are in 1 to 2 tsp and tbsp., and 1 cup.
Season to your own taste using this guide)
Goat from your local butcher
Salt & Pepper
Garlic Powder
Onion Powder
Curry Powder
Ground Allspice
Potato
Butter Beans
Scotch Bonnet Pepper (optional)
Fresh herbs – ginger, rosemary, thyme

Rinse the goat under cool water
Season the meat with dry seasoning
Add onions and peppers, let sit for at least 1 hour
Add oil to a pot and increase heat to high
Add goat meat and braise until browned
Add water or beef broth
Cover and reduce heat
Cook covered for 4 hours (checking every hour)
3rd hour add potatoes and butter beans
Return cover and cook through until tender
Boil your rice per package instructions
Serve hot!

Pan Seared Chicken w/red beans & rice

(Measurements are in 1 to 2 tsp and tbsp., and 1 cup.
Season to your own taste using this guide)
Chicken Legs or Quarters
Garlic Powder
Onion Powder
Salt & Pepper
Vegetable Seasoning
Olive Oil
Rice
Red Beans
Beef or Pork Sausage

Chicken:
Clean chicken with cold water and rinse with white vinegar
Rinse vinegar and add the dry seasoning
Let sit for at least an hour
Add oil to pan and sear chicken; keep pan uncovered
Add chicken broth to pan if liquid reduces to avoid burning

Rice:
Soak dry red kidney beans over night
if using can red kidney beans, drain and rinse
Bring pot of water to a boil
Add beans
When water reduces and beans are tender add chicken broth
Add rice to the pot and cook around red beans
Add cooked sausage to red beans (optional)

Lake Michigan Chicago Illinois

Every June I find myself in Chicago Ill working during the day and bar hopping during the night. Chicago is one jumping city, they offer bar upon bar upon bar, the city never sleeps. I love that they sell liquor in 7/11 so I don't need to find a liquor store just to get my buzz.

Just as there are many offerings to wet your whistle there are equally, if not more, places to eat and party in downtown Chicago. Each time I visit I find a new place that I absolutely love. Chicago boast their different styles of hot dogs and let me tell you I have tried many and they were all absolutely tasty and wonderful!.Can you tell that I love the Chicago area?

I plan to be in Chicago again in June 2017, to do my traditional bar hopping tour. Meet me there!

Easy Pan Seared Chicken w/Mushrooms

(Measurements are in 1 to 2 tsp and tbsp., and 1 cup.
Season to your own taste using this guide)
Our cover recipe - Easy Pan Seared Chicken w/Mushrooms
Chicken legs, thighs, or quarters
Mushrooms
Cilantro (in the Caribbean we call this Shadow Benny)
Onions
Peppers
Chicken Broth
Garlic & Onion Powder
Vegetable seasoning

Clean chicken with cool water then soak in vinegar
Thoroughly rinse vinegar off chicken then pat dry
Season chicken with dry seasoning
Add onions & peppers to chicken
Let sit for about an hour
Add oil to a heated pan
Place chicken in pan and sear (or some call it braising)
Add chicken broth and water (do not cover)
Add mushrooms to the pan
Brown chicken until water and broth evaporates

Fish stuffed with mushrooms & peppers

The Hill Center Washington DC

Washington DC is a mecca for culture with its unique areas of distinct tastes. China Town delivers the most authentic Asian cuisine while the downtown area provides many choices from exquisite food trucks to amazing seafood pulled right of the Chesapeake bay.

With the many offerings if one is looking for a unique DC taste you must try the chicken wings and mambo sauce, a DC unique specialty! Many around the country boast their chicken wings but none comes close to this local recipe. If you ever find yourself in the DC area chicken wings and mambo sauce is just around every corner.

Aside from the obvious seafood like the amazing Maryland Crab Cakes, you have to try the food vendor trucks all over downtown DC. I know many travelers who come to DC make visiting the hot dog vendor trucks a part of their travel plans.

Braised Cabbage

(Measurements are in 1 to 2 tsp and tbsp., and 1 cup.
Season to your own taste using this guide)
Head of cabbage
Carrots
Onions & Peppers
Salt & Pepper
Chicken or Vegetable broth

Rinse and cut cabbage head into thin slices
Add olive oil to pan on high heat
Add cabbage to oil and stir
Stir for about 2 minutes and add onions and green peppers
Add sliced carrots
Season with salt & pepper
When oil evaporates add broth and stir until braised

JW Marriott Phoenix Arizona

Chicken Salad Wrap

You'll need chicken breast, mayonnaise, shredded cheese, bacon, salt & pepper, and lettuce
Unwrap chicken and clean thoroughly
In a cast iron pan place oil in pan and add the chicken breast
cover and cook through on medium heat about 45 min.
Once cooked cut the chicken breast up into small cubed pieces
Add chicken to bowl
Stir in mayonnaise, onions, bell peppers, salt and pepper

Plating: place a whole leaf romaine lettuce on a plate
Fill with chicken mixture
Sprinkle on shredded cheese
Add crispy bacon (optional)

Miami Florida

Seafood Platter

Creamy Potato and Mushroom Soup

(Measurements are in 1 to 2 tsp and tbsp., and 1 cup. Season to your own taste using this guide)
2-4 Potatoes
1 cup mushrooms
1 large white onion
1 large red onion
1 cup shredded carrots
2-4 clove garlic
1 cup all-purpose flower
½ cup milk or heavy cream
1 cup chicken broth
2 strips bacon
Salt & pepper
Cajun seasoning

In a medium to large pan cook bacon
When bacon is fully cooked remove and set aside
Chop white onions and garlic
Place carrots, onion and garlic in bacon grease and cook down until onion is translucent
Pour in chicken broth and stir to mix thoroughly
In small pot add flower and pour in milk – mix until smooth
Pour flower mixture into pot with chicken broth
Add potatoes and mushrooms
Turn heat down to low and cover
Cook for about 20-30 minutes
Pour half of the soup into a food compressor and pulse until liquid is smooth
Pour back into pot and stir with remaining soup
Add salt and pepper to taste
Garnish with your choice of cheese, red onion, and remaining bacon

I'm very picky about where I eat and whose food I eat. I guess being in the kitchen and on the other side of the table so often it made me appreciate my own food. I love when Thanksgiving comes around because my mom is the best cook to me. Her holiday meals I wait patiently for all year. My mom and dad and my sisters are my food critics. Whenever I try something new I always let one of them taste it before I start advertising it. One thing I have noticed is we as people tend to take short cuts when cooking. I've seen people not wash their meats and not season their food. This is dangerous for one, the meat could be contaminated by sitting in its own fluids for how long we really don't know. Two, seasoning your food for at least an hour makes your meal taste so much better. Growing up I used to see my mom season beef or chicken on Saturday to cook on Sunday. It's OK to season people, just clean it first!

Spicy Southwestern Rolls

You may find this hard to believe or better yet never even given it a thought. Your mood or how happy you feel makes your dishes come out so much better, why because your happy. Just like the feeling of love makes you feel giddy inside and makes you smile for no reason at all, well the way we enter into the kitchen and begin to prepare food that same giddiness will transfer into what your cooking. Try it one day for yourself you'll find that when you were feeling very happy and good about yourself that was the day whatever you made turned out really good. Those days that were rough on us we can probably remember not feeling good about what we ate that night most likely because it was rushed or it was just something to get us by. Whenever I am cooking for a large group of people or an important occasion I try to keep my mood positive and my attitude great because I know the importance it will have on my final creations.

Smoked Salmon & Avocado Bagel

(Measurements are in 1 to 2 tsp and tbsp., and 1 cup.
Season to your own taste using this guide)
Bagel
Smoked Salmon
Ripe Avocado
Onions
Capers
Cream Cheese
Lemon Juice
Salt & Pepper

Toast bagels in oven or toaster oven
Spread cream cheese onto toasted bagel
Add smoked salmon
top with avocado, onions, and capers
Drizzle with lemon juice, salt & pepper to taste

Spicy Thai Noodles

Stuffed Chicken Breast

(Measurements are in 1 to 2 tsp and tbsp., and 1 cup.
Season to your own taste using this guide)
Two Chicken Breast
Spinach
Cream Cheese
Whipping cream
Salt & Pepper
Garlic & Onion Powder
Tomatoes

Season chicken breast well
Place in refrigerator for at least an hour
Spinach mix: add to a bowl cream cheese, whipping cream, and cooked spinach
Pan sear the chicken breast in the olive oil
Once cooked remove the chicken
Wait until manageable by touch
Add the spinach mix to the chicken
Place chicken breast in preheated oven for about 30 minutes
Season diced tomatoes with olive oil and basil
Top chicken with seasoned diced tomatoes
Season with salt & pepper to taste
Serve hot!

New Stanton Pennsylvania

Garlic Butter Shrimp & Pasta

(Measurements are in 1 to 2 tsp and tbsp., and 1 cup. Season to your own taste using this guide)
Shrimp
Garlic
Butter
Olive oil
Black pepper
Fresh parsley
Cajun seasoning
Pasta

In a medium pot boil pasta noodles as directed
In a medium pot boil the shrimp until they become nice and pink
Drain and let cool
Remove shell and season with butter, garlic, and Cajun seasoning
Toss to coat
Plate pasta adding the shrimp and drizzle with garlic butter sauce

San Diego, California

San Diego California! Need I say more? The area is full of the most sexiest people on the planet, at least so I figure. My wife and I spent a week in the area and never once saw an out of shape person nor an unattractive woman or man, it was incredible! Being from Washington DC we weren't used to watching football at 10am in the morning let alone sitting in a sports-bar drinking beer and rooting for our favorite teams but it happened. So here I am in a Mexican sports-bar drinking Coronas and dipping chips in guacamole and staring at several big screen TV's, I was in heaven, at least so I thought until the beautiful waitress came by with a special tequila shot menu. My wife is the tequila drinker and her eyes lit up lol. Not far from the Mexican border we enjoyed all types of authentic Mexican dishes and drinks. If you're ever in the area I suggest the Gaslamp District, you won't be disappointed.

Crawfish aka

Crawdads, Crayfish, Mudbugs, Crays

Lobster Tail in Garlic Butter

Journey. It has a profound meaning. It Is the path we embark upon without Knowing its' destination. It's all the Experiences we face and welcome. It's where we find Love, Laughter, and above all....Great Food!

Bay Village, Lake Erie Ohio

Elkridge Community Chicago ILL

Author & Chef Winston Cayne Clarke
2016-2017